A Sampler of Uncommon Sense and Good Times/Emotional Trips, Whimsy and More in Rhymes

Poems That Say What They Mean in Rhyme

George L. Hand

iUniverse, Inc.
Bloomington

A Sampler of Uncommon Sense and Good Times/ Emotional Trips, Whimsy and More in Rhymes
Poems That Say What They Mean in Rhyme

iUniverse books may be ordered through booksellers or by contacting:

iUniverse
1663 Liberty Drive
Bloomington, IN 47403
www.iuniverse.com
1-800-Authors (1-800-288-4677)

Because of the dynamic nature of the Internet, any web addresses or links contained in this book may have changed since publication and may no longer be valid. The views expressed in this work are solely those of the author and do not necessarily reflect the views of the publisher, and the publisher hereby disclaims any responsibility for them.

Any people depicted in stock imagery provided by Thinkstock are models, and such images are being used for illustrative purposes only.

Certain stock imagery © Thinkstock.

ISBN: 978-1-4502-8783-8 (sc)
ISBN: 978-1-4502-8784-5 (ebk)

Printed in the United States of America

iUniverse rev. date: 01/14/2011

This book is dedicated to our nine grand daughters and one grand son.

Laura, Lindsay, Kimberly, Elizabeth, Aileen, Kathryn, Shaylynn, Brian, Lucy, and Victoria

Contents

1. Old Is Not So Bad (Considering the Alternative)

Old Is Okay

Old friends, old wines, old memories, old times.
Many things are revered with age.
Old coins, old glory, old masters, old story.
Old is a great word, so says the old sage.

Remembrance

If we are amongst the lucky ones,
We'll be remembered by our daughters and sons.
If they marry and reproduce in time,
Some grand kids may remember us from our prime.
Will they remember us for things we've done?
Or are we the old duffers who once were fun.
We may think famous people in the public eye
Will have enough fame to be remembered by.
But who really knows about Lincoln's life,
Or his personal feelings, known only to his wife.
Shakespeare, the greatest, known by any other name,
Would still be unknown, no matter his fame.
I'm afraid our station in life now and here
Will mean nothing to most people in less than a year.
We'll only be remembered by those we love,
And that will just last 'til they pass up above.

Running

At our age we have to change how we talk.
Everywhere we'd normally say "run," it's now "walk."
"Well, we have to walk," when we're in a hurry to go.
"We're walking a few errands," at our age we're slow.
Will anyone salute, if we walk this up the pole?
Do we walk something by the boss? How droll.
Here's hoping we don't have to walk each machine,
Or walk the bath, if you know what I mean.
Walking for public office, we don't do it's agreed
The rest of the world needn't slow to our speed.
We have our own rate which we won't exceed.

Time Travel

Time has confused folks from ages past.
How do you define it? The question has been asked.
It doesn't exist modern physicists may claim,
Though the average person doesn't play that game.
We can order events. What came first we know,
And our lives unwind for us from the very get go.
We also know that the past is different from the now,
And will be different from the future though we know
not how.
We know that travel in time can't be done.
We can't travel forward or back, neither one.
However, what we can do is remember back,
And relive in our minds if we have the knack.
We have past experiences in our brains you see.
That is our time travel. For us it can be.

Still

We've come to that point we can call the "still" age.
It starts when people ask, "Are you still earning a wage?"
Then about health," Are you still limping on that knee,
Or has it been replaced? You're still dancing I see."
Later, "Are you still driving that big old car?"
What they really mean, "Are you still driving that far?"
"That house you love, are you still living there,
Or have you moved where they provide full care?"
It appears they'll ask and ask until,
It comes to the point that you are "still."

Rosie's Way

Macho, macho man, only do those manly things.
Make sure you never show what softness brings.
Gotta make the other guys think you're tough.
Swear, drink, and smoke. Do that macho stuff.
Thank God for men like Roosevelt Greer.
For our pro defensive lineman, we can cheer.
He liked needlepoint. For him it was relaxing.
In no way was this hobby taxing.
Now that we're old we can follow his lead.
Forgetting that macho stuff can be our creed.
Want to sing, then sing, want to paint, then paint.
We're still men, though macho we ain't.
To hell with all those who're afraid to try,
Do something that's new before you die.

Tears

When you're a kid it's okay to show tears.
It becomes less okay with the passage of years.
With our kids we had a rule of sorts.
Emotions or a hit in the nose from sports,
Was reason enough to shed a tear or two,
But not for ordinary hurts as they grew.
As the Bible says, when a child becomes a man,
He puts away childish things. That's the plan.
The rule still holds for adults, you see.
You just don't cry from injury.
However, I find as the years pass by,
Emotions bring tears. The eyes don't stay dry.

Why

We need something and get up from the chair,
But forget what it was after climbing upstairs.
The lament that's said with no cheer.
"Dear Lord, why am I here?"
Why do we forget? It's nature at play.
Retrace our steps. More exercise that way.

Activities

When you're retired, you have this choice.
You can try what you want. You should rejoice.
To keep you busy, there are uncounted things,
So there's no excuse not to take a few flings.
If you don't like what you've chosen to do,
You can stop and try something else that's new.
With all the choices, it's up to you.

Eyesight

The lovely young lass after all these years
Is just the same as she always appears.
The benefit of failing eyesight when old,
You can't see true love's wrinkles I'm told.

Getting Up

No pain in the morning,
When getting out of bed?
Take it as a warning,
You're probably dead.

Why Me?

The calendar says I'm getting old.
I don't feel it so much, if I may be so bold.
For balance I need neither walker nor cane.
My maladies are pretty mild in the main.
A few age spots and some wrinkly skin
Are outward signs of the shape I'm in.
With relatives and acquaintances feeling their age,
Why me, Lord? Why such luck at this life's stage?

Blank

When we walk into another room,
We're hit with thoughts of gloom.
We've forgotten what we've come here for.
Our minds go blank at the door.
It's okay, we'll remember again
After sitting down back in the den.

Feeling Fine

When asked, how are you, most answer fine.
This comes out naturally. We don't want to whine.
We may be in hospital with tubes in and out,
Or just getting up from a sickness bout.
I answer, "Fair to middling," when it's true.
But not if in a really bad way and feeling blue.
The answer, most don't really want to know,
So, "Fine" will do. Don't tell them your woe.

Gravity Always Wins

With gravity we have a lifetime fight.
Though it's unfortunate, it is our plight.
From our earliest days, the lesson we learn,
Gravity wins. It's a law we cannot spurn.
Little tykes find with balance lost, you fall down.
It matters little if you squall or frown.
Gravity still affects us old duffers too.
Loose skin pulls down, this is always true.
At least it doesn't gather around each shoe.

No Change

At the fiftieth class reunion you meet.
Haven't seen each other. She says something sweet.
"Why in all this time, you haven't changed a bit."
Unlikely, but translated, "I recognize you," will fit.
For kids, teens, adults, and the old reprobate,
Time flies by at the same rapid rate.

No Complaints

"How are you?" "Oh, I have this pain.
All things considered, I can't complain.
Compared with the alternative, I should say, quite well.
Thus, on my mild condition, I will not dwell."

The Trick

We all have that big memory lapse.
For young people they appear as mental gaps.
Where are the keys? Or more important where's the car.
At least you don't have to wonder where you are.
As age advances, the problem becomes worse.
You may walk away and forget your purse.
You forget a key word. You forget a name.
You are embarrassed, but for all it's the same.
There is one trick that will give you a clue.
Just consciously be aware of what you do.
Repeat to yourself, I am putting my keys here.
I'm parking my car by that door I'm near.
I'm getting up to get a paper and pen.
I went to do a chore. That's where I've been.
Maybe talking to yourself seems sort of odd.
It's okay, since you're not talking to God.
If you slip up and talk to the air,
Don't worry cause cell phones are everywhere.

Falling

When you're old, pay attention all the time.
Make some concessions. You're not in your prime.
Kids can fall many times without getting hurt.
They're supple and fairly close to the dirt.
We old ones aren't agile, and we're easy to break.
So know where you're stepping for goodness sake.

Try

I address this to the old, especially the men.
You used to work, now you're free, so amen.
There are so many things for you to try.
Why just sit around and wait to die?

Gone

Here today, gone tomorrow,
Is a phrase that I must borrow.
How long will we remember,
Maybe not past next December?
That's a thought to bring you sorrow.

Old Animals

Old is never a problem amongst our wild kin.
When they lose a step, their life chances dim.
Maybe other members of their tribe
Will help with food to keep them alive.
When they no longer can get to the water hole,
Then in a few days, thirst will take its toll.
Chances they'll die, if they're sick or hurt.

We see no old wild animals, I can assert.
For domesticated ones, it's a different tale.
Their age doesn't show, though they're not so hale.
A few grey whiskers and a sway back,
But of wrinkly skin there is a lack.
Nor do they have a baldness attack.

I'm Glad
More than one old person I've heard say,
I'm glad I was born back in my day.
Life was less complicated along the way.
Less harried and much more fun if I may.

Be Strong
Old age doesn't come by itself for sure.
We seem to get enough maladies to endure
Thus, we can say old age is for the strong.
You have to take it, or you won't be here long.
The alternative, of course, is to leave while young.
Given that choice, with the old I'll be among.

Aging
Amongst the animals, years don't show much rampage.
Just people seem to show their age.
Loss of hair and wrinkles are the gauge.

Surprise

Why I'm so surprised. How big you've grown.
But then I must observe, so have my own.
We've grown older, it's not an aging race.
It seems time flows for all at the same pace.

Alternative

Life is good. There may be some pain
But on the whole, we shouldn't complain.
If the alternative, we'd just consider,
About our ailments, we'd each be a kidder.

Choose

There is some advice I wish to give.
Knowing the alternative, choose to live.
Life or death when you have a choice,
Sing it out with a loud, clear voice.
I choose life. In this I rejoice.

No Immunity

As we grow older maybe we learn
About the saying which we usually spurn.
We're not immune, it is our fate.
Old too soon, smart too late.

2. Heroics

The Landing

John was drafted back in forty three.

He wasn't the type to volunteer, you see.

He had thought he'd work at a ship building job.

His was an ordinary family. He wasn't a snob.

In basic training he worked his butt off.

He threw up a few times, but please don't scoff.

John always tried as hard as he could.

His body might give out. His mind never would.

As luck would have it, he became a grunt.

The Army needed young men for the front.

The first and most important thing he learned,

This fact on each soldier's brain is burned,

Your best friend is your rifle, no doubt.

Often it's the only thing to help you out.

Take care of it. It will take care of you.

For a GI this fact is always true.

John joined a unit, to England it was sent.

Training continued, all their time was so spent.

Especially, they learned about landing craft.

Maybe to ride on one, you had to be daft.

While waiting in England, John had time to think.

Would the craft take a hit leaving men in the drink?

His thoughts always came back to a common fear.

Would he be brave when death was near?

Most every soldier thinks along this line.
They'd hope and pray they'd have the spine.
The thought of letting their buddies down,
They'd rather put themselves in the ground.
In early June, arrived the big day.
It was before dawn. The sky was gray.
Approaching the beach, the boat stopped on a swell.
The ramp dropped, and the men entered hell.
John like many, never made it out of the boat.
Did he have the right stuff? John, please take note.
We know and God knows you were a hero that day.
"It was meant to be," is all we can say.
The poor guy never had a chance to know,
Brave or not, death took him in tow.
A hero nevertheless, this honor we can bestow.

Behind the Lines

He boarded the plane just after dark.
They flew southeast, on the map there was a mark.
He had to trust the flight crew on this.
He sure hoped the drop zone, they wouldn't miss.
Going behind the lines, he'd be on his own.
Maybe he's odd, but he'd rather be alone.
He much preferred this to landing on the beach.
A thousand guns aimed as they charged into the breach.
The typical GI on those landing craft
Preferred that mission. They thought he was daft.
He was dressed like a French peasant. They'd call him a spy.
If he ever got captured, no Geneva rules apply.

If he wore a uniform, he'd be a prisoner of war.
He didn't think the Germans would care anymore.
Either soldier or spy, he'd be just as dead.
No mention of his mission would ever be read.
He had to make contact with the resistance below.
His mission was to tell them what bridges to blow.
It was important to all those going ashore
To limit reinforcements to a trickle, no more.
They're on approach. The pilot flashed the light.
The door was opened. He went into the night.
No one will ever know how many GIs were saved.
All those who participated took that knowledge to the grave.
It's one of thousands of stories never told.
How ordinary men were both brave and bold.

Snipers

In the European theater during World War Two,
The GI's were a rather inventive crew.
It seems the Germans while retreating toward home
Often would leave a sniper behind all alone.
He would cause our advance to slow down
By firing from a concealed position in town.
Then someone had an idea so bold
It seamed so obvious, no one had to be sold.
A 155 cannon, they brought to the front.
It was fired point blank. The building took the brunt.
The Germans complained. This must be against the rules.
Did they think that we were just a bunch of fools?
No city building was worth one boy's life.

Tough, but that's what happens in war strife.
There was no need to worry about civilian loss.
To get out of the way or face death was their cross.
Why can't we use techniques like that now?
Can we return fire to save our own? No how.
We should spread the word with every breath.
The civilians' job is to choose, vacate or face death.

The Pilot

The old man had not flown for a while.
This was his final mission, he thought with a smile.
He flew naval planes long ago in the war.
That was another life, way back in forty four.
Once he ditched in the sea after taking some flak.
He got out okay with his raft in its pack.
Survival wasn't certain with the ocean so vast.
How many days would his water supply last?
Luck was with him, more than most who flew.
A Polynesian fisherman found him with his canoe.
From that day on all his life was a gift.
He always gave back. He was never adrift.
Now his wife of many decades was dead.
His kids, with the grand kids, were happily wed.
After his last checkup with the final day news,
He got everything in order. He'd paid all his dues.
Now in his closing days, a decision was made.
He would travel back. His determination wouldn't fade.
He would set himself adrift on the wide sea.
"My circle of life will be complete," thought he.

He knew his island and was transported there.
This was the place where his life was spared.
The native fisherman listened to his plan.
No one would help him, it was taboo to their clan.
The fisherman explained what the old ones do,
When they can no longer fish and paddle a canoe.
They sit on the beach and watch the seas.
They tell stories to the young under the trees.
The sunset's glory, nature's bounty, a land with no strife.
That's how they continue the circle of life.
The old man thought, but not for long.
It's a better way to go. It can't be wrong.
Better with a story on your lips, singing life's song.

Submarines

They left Pearl Harbor late in the day.
The sub could travel more safely that way.
Most thought submerged was always the norm.
At night the surface was safe except in a storm.
Close to Hawaii the danger's from our own.
One flyboy mistake, and from the water they'd be blown.
They traveled northwest to the Japanese isles,
And took up station and waited awhile.
The waiting was hard in the sub's cramped space.
Some of the young wondered, "Why this place?"
Soon they learned the mission for the sub.
The sonar detected passing ships up above.
Japan needed the materials transported by sea.
Sink the ships bringing supplies, was the sub's decree.

They raised periscope and took careful aim.
A spread of torpedoes soon ended the game.
This worked fine until the fateful day.
A destroyer quietly waited, then got under way.
The sub dived as fast as it could.
Depth charges exploded right where it stood.
The men died quickly as the sub sank.
Their bodies were crushed independent of rank.
Though these sailors' graves will never be found,
We all know their strategic mission was sound.
Japan was starving for material at war's end.
The submarine force was the cause of this trend.
They died heroes doing more than their share.
Now on eternal patrol, they have our prayers.

Straight and Level
The Dakotas were all spaced in a line.
If a general viewed it, he'd think it was fine.
Three at a time they approached the drop zone.
Hundreds of planes, but they each felt alone.
The commander said fly level and straight.
No evasive tactics to avoid the eighty-eight.
This was the all-purpose German artillery gun.
All that flak is what they'd like to shun.
The commander said it was a matter of chance
Whether you went straight or did an aerial dance.
Your odds of a hit were about the same
So flying straight was the name of the game.
The drop zone was an area of grass.

The nearby swamps and woods they should pass.
The airborne troops were in their care.
To the right spot, they'd get them there.
Straight and level until the shell hit.
Don't lose control. Get that jump light lit.
The last man was barely out the door.
The pilot did his job. You could ask for no more.
It was much too late to leave the plane.
He flew it straight in, but he didn't die in vain.
Maybe each of these pilots wasn't a well known star,
But among the heroes, they had no par.

On the Beach

They had been pinned on the beach for more than an hour.
The men couldn't move. The results had been dour.
The surf moved the bodies both wounded and dead.
The survivors would join them unless they were led.
All the young officers , their leaders, were gone.
They had succumbed to enemy fire soon after dawn.
The few sergeants tried to rally the troops.
They were spread on the beach in isolated groups.
In time they all would certainly be dead.
"Follow us up the embankment and charge instead.
If you're going to die, then die like a man.
Kill a few Nazis. Get them while you can."
It made some sense, what the Sarge had said.
Some, then more, conquered their dread.
Over the wall, then on up the beach.
Charge up that path, the Nazis to reach.

The enemy had connecting trenches to each pill box.
Their positions were strong with these interlocks.
Some of the men were blasted by mines,
And cross fire came from several lines.
The GIs fell on the left and on the right.
Those who remained continued to fight.
A few, then more, reached the top of the bluff.
They fired and threw grenades, but was it enough?
Then suddenly the defenders started to appear.
Their hands were in the air. A GI gave a cheer.
"Kamerad," they yelled, a surrender call.
One GI wouldn't allow it. He shot them all.
"My buddies on the beach," he explained as he killed,
Had no chance to surrender as their lives were stilled."
Was this justice? No one can say.
But it happened more than once on that day.

LST

The sailors renamed this noble sea going tub.
"Long Slow Target," a ship only its mother could love.
The Landing Ship Tank had to get close to the shore.
When they ran aground, they opened the door.
Tanks and the heavy equipment could drive right out.
With these, the troops on the beach had more clout.
Normally, the beach should be secured when they land.
On D-Day the invasion hardly went as planned.
The enemy on the heights could rain down fire.
When the ships came close, the results could be dire.
"To hell with the fire, full steam ahead,"

Said the Captain. For them there was certainly dread.
They dropped anchor well before going aground.
Then blasted up on the beach with a grinding sound.
The tanks drove off. They returned enemy fire.
The GIs now had close support to inspire.
The enemy pill boxes couldn't take direct hits.
Our troops stormed forward gaining ground in bits.
Each LST had to vacate its landing spot.
Dropping the anchor was part of this plot.
Each ship pulled its anchor chain. Full speed astern.
They got out of the way, the next ship had its turn.
The LST wasn't designed to land in a fight,
But by God these men showed the Navy's might.
The men on the beach needed their support.
They did their job. They wouldn't come up short.

The Chapel

The troops had been walking for more than a day.
The rest of the division was well on its way.
The German army was retreating back toward home.
Our rapid pursuit had left some units alone.
Leaders are supposed to take care of their men.
That's why they stopped at the chapel in the glen.
Lieutenant Bob tried to find if they could rest there,
But no one was around who seemed to care.
An older couple appeared and saw their plight.
They said the chapel could be used for the night.
The couple brought food. The place was snug and warm.
All were happy and full, far from any harm.

The next morning Bob wanted to express their thanks.
He hailed a passing farmer whose expression was blank.
"Oh, you must have met Marie and Jacques.
They show up when there's a reason to come back.
You see, they both died about 28 years ago.
An errant shell from the Germans delivered the blow.
Now, to help, they do anything they can."
"But we were fed to the very last man.
There was coffee and milk, fresh bread and cheese.
The stew with real meat brought the men to their knees.
How is this possible in this day and age?"
"Just accept what is," replied the old sage.

Kwajalein (to my grandson)
The Navy and Army had a plan in the Pacific.
It was called island hopping to be specific.
Choose an island on which you could build a base.
Let the Japs occupy every other place.
Our Navy could keep their navy at bay.
The occupied islands would be no threat this way.
Their troops could get no resupply.
They were left all alone waiting to die.
The island, Kwajalein, is part of an atoll.
Of the atoll islands, it played a pivotal roll.
Kwaj' is pretty isolated, just north of the equator,
Equidistant from Hawaii and Japan, you locate her.
At the end of January back in forty four
B-24s and naval guns battered her shore.
Each fortification blasted, no standing palm tree.

Most was destroyed in the bombing spree.

The Marines took Roi-Namur, the Army took Kwaj'.

Mostly it was mopping up after the barrage.

It was successfully over, after only four days.

One of the least costly of the Pacific forays.

Still almost four hundred brave souls died

To secure the atoll for the use of our side.

The Japs lost almost twenty times this count,

Thus proving the advantage of the bombardment amount.

The islands had radar sets after the war.

Grandpa visited there for his job. I can't say more.

Roi-Namur still had relics 23 years later.

Tanks, amphibious and land, and defenses cratered.

While walking the beach looking for shells

I found these casings not removed by ocean swells.

I want you to have these from a far away sea,

A reminder of the men who helped keep us free.

We can hope the Marine whose casings I found there

Returned to his family, his life being spared.

The Destroyers

On D-Day over 5000 ships were off the beach.

A German observer saw the armada and lost his speech.

All he could think, looking near and far.

We can't withstand this. We've lost the war.

There were dozens of types of ship and boat.

Among them was the destroyer, one of the most sleek afloat.

Their job was to protect the fleet from attack.

From German air in front or U-boats in back.

They patrolled near the shore since the fleet was safe.
No air attacks from bombs or planes that strafe.
The Captain said, "We've got to help those ashore.
Pull in closer. We must do more."
"But Captain, our orders are to protect the fleet.
Besides, we can run aground. Then we'll get the heat."
"The hell with that, Those men are in need."
The destroyer charged forward at full speed.
"But we have no targets. We can't see our men.
Are they on the bluff? Can we fire and when?'
The wind blew the smoke. Then they could see.
The men were still on the beach. They hadn't broken free.
The destroyer blasted the bluff, then someone saw.
The tanks were shooting near the draw.
"All guns on that target," the Captain yelled.
Every gun of the ship created a hell.
The gunners relied on where the tanks fired.
They even spotted targets the riflemen acquired.
One ship ran parallel to the beach at full speed,
Blasting away to help the GIs in need.
Then it stopped and ran full speed astern,
Blasting again without bothering to turn
Another case where heroes acted on their own,
No orders needed. They decided and did it alone.
At least three ships, the Harding, Frankfort, and McCook,
Did their part, no worry about the chances they took.
When they retired after doing their part,
Every magazine was empty. They were full at the start.
This was a great example for an Army-Navy game.
There may be rivalry, but the men are the same.

Who Were Those GIs

When I was a kid, they were ten feet tall.
By modern standards they seem pretty small.
Five feet eight and rather thin they were.
At one hundred forty four, there wasn't much there.
In pictures I've seen, they were slender but fit.
You could describe them as wiry with true grit.
The average GI put on seven pounds of muscle
While going through the basic training tussle.
Often they went into battle with a 50 pound pack,
Except when they needed more on their back.
About half were high school grads or more.
This made them the best educated Army by far.
These were the kids who grew up down the street.
They overcame any obstacle they came to meet.
It's said that we won due to industrial might.
I prefer the reason, our young men could fight.
They'll always be the greatest heroes in my sight.

Our Boys

How I feel about our troops, you're certainly aware.
I'm not the only one in the world who so cares.
In forty five, most armies were the cause of dread.
On their approach everyone who could, fled.
When they arrived, it meant looting and rape.
Senseless destruction and killing if you didn't escape.
This was certainly true of the Germans and Japs.
The Red Army were known to be murderous chaps.
In contrast, after the enemy retreated from each place,

Our arriving GIs were accepted with smiles on each face.
Our Army meant freedom and the three Cs,
Candy, cigarettes, and C-rations given free.
Often GIs would save food of their own,
So they could give to the kids and those full grown.
They came not to conquer, but to liberate.
We sent our best, the people could celebrate.
In the future they'd be known as the greatest generation.
They should continue to have our complete veneration.

Second Guessing

It's dark. The patrol moves down the road.
The adrenalin is pumping. They're on full alert mode.
The lead sees movement out of the corner of his eye.
His brain registers danger. He doesn't want to die.
His weapon's on automatic. His body is too.
He turns and instantly decides what to do.
Without careful aim he lets go a blast.
A body crumples forward and breaths his last.
It's a middle aged man with a stick in his hand.
He's dressed like everyone else in this land.
Should the soldier hesitate a bit and be shot,
Or react as he did without thinking a lot.
Some would charge him with murder for his action,
Though they would likely have the same reaction.
Can you judge such a man in a quiet room,
When you never have felt his reaction to doom.
Please don't second guess our military men.
They don't have the choice of the where or the when.

The War

When people my age and older say, "The war,"
There's no need to explain, no need to say more.
For the twentieth century, this was the defining event.
A whole generation knew what total war meant.
Ours and other nations stood up in that fight.
We defeated two evil regimes with our might.
There was no doubt about what was right.

The Pledge

If you're running to be a congressional rep,
You need to take a very important step.
The same applies to senators from each state,
And most important each presidential candidate.
Take this oath before God and man.
"I will never send American troops to some foreign land
And put them in a position most dire.
Where they cannot return enemy fire."
It should be up to the soldier on the spot
Whether he risks his own life or not.
No politician or general is being shot.

Who's a Hero

There's some confusion on both how a hero is made,
And the difference between courage and being afraid.
A hero can have fear as anyone would
When facing a situation that's not so good.
An excellent swimmer can save a kid in a lake.
He's not a true hero for goodness sake.
There is no fear to overcome with this deed.

Though, he's a good person, it must be agreed.
A lousy swimmer though, would be a hero here.
On entering the water, he conquered his fear.
A true hero overcomes fear and even faces death.
He tries to do the right thing to his very last breath.
Supermen is not a hero, since there's no reason to fear.
Taking care of bad guys is his normal career.
Nor are sportsmen heroes for playing with pain.
They know the bench beckons if there's nothing to gain.
For hero I pick the average Joe who stands out,
And risks his life with the outcome in doubt.

The Vets

Being a kid at the end of the war,
I knew who were my heroes and more.
The men who stood the highest in my eyes
Were the vets, the unmatched American GIs.

Other Heroes

Some may be so depressed, it's hard to function.
They carry on anyway because of their gumption
Sometimes heroism is showing up each day
When it would be easier to just stay away.
You do it because you're needed, some would say.

3. Philosophical Thoughts

Why Poetry?

Read poetry, write poetry, you must be nuts.
Real men are too macho, no ifs, ands, or buts.
Poetry is for women and each artsy type.
Why would you read that kind of tripe?
And yet:
Every song has the meter, including rap,
And many are rhyming, our fingers we snap.
So it's okay for a macho guy, a poem to sing.
Just don't catch him reading like some ding-a-ling.
Actually, poetry can be rewarding to read.
Like in the songs, there's emotions to heed.
It occasionally provides the fun that we need.

Defining Me

It seems we are defined by our relation to others.
At birth we're a son and maybe a brother.
Grandson, nephew, and cousin we may add.
With age there are husband, uncle, and dad.
Some definitions are earned by what we do.
Often we get this answer from, "What are you?"
Do you define yourself by ethnicity or race,
Or the country you live in or some other place?
We're defined by religion, the church we attend,

Our political party, or how much money we spend.
With all these definitions, you should pick your own.
Don't let someone else decide how you're known.
The ones I cherish will last to the end.
These are the combination of father, husband, lover, and friend.

Color Red
Red in nature is pretty rare around here.
Though some pink flowers give us cheer.
No mammals, reptiles or insects are red.
Just a few birds like the woodpecker's head.
We have a cardinal family that visits us.
The robin red breast is more the color of rust.
So when I think of red, it's the color of blood.
Mostly it's no problem lest it comes in a flood.
Like when the boy hits the stone wall. He doesn't cry,
But calmly asks, "Am I going to die?"
"No my son, but we'll check it out."
The emergency doctor removes any doubt.
I've bled a few times, usually from careless ways,
When I try to defy gravity and then I pay.
One sight of blood should give us cheer,
When the Red Cross comes, it's mission is clear.
Bleed a little bit to help some unknown live.
Red is the color of the life we give.

Definition

When I read the obits, I haven't a clue.

I wonder why they define us as they do.

John Smith survived by his loving wife,

With all descendants. What a brief summary of his life.

No mention of death's cause or his age.

What did he do to earn his wage?

Maybe country of birth and its date.

Schools he attended. Where did he meet his mate.

Military service or other special things he's done.

Did he volunteer? What did he do for fun?

From the given facts, what can we tell?

If he had great grand kids, he lived pretty well.

If he was survived by siblings and mom and dad,

Then it's a sure sign of an ending that's sad.

Maybe it's not my business, this personal stuff.

Maybe the obit's definition of the guy is enough.

Thoreau in the Know

In a lot of respects, Thoreau was a fake.
Staying overnight in jail does not a hero make.
Suffering for your beliefs when there's hardly any pain.
Doesn't justify preaching the civil disobedience refrain.
Living in a cabin while accepting gifts free
Hardly counts as living independent of society.
However, he had a good point about stuff.
We really have much more than enough.
Simplify is Thoreau's lesson; we all should learn.
All of life's clutter is what we should spurn.
Fancy cars and houses and all their filling
Make us slaves, though we're perfectly willing.
He called it a life of quiet desperation.
We have a choice. Thoreau's our inspiration.

Maverick

Lived so many years ago,
A social critic we should know,
The maverick named Thoreau,
Preached simplify. Complexity is our foe.

Pain

When the well meaning person recites the refrain,
"I know what you're feeling. I share your pain."
We'd like to say bull, but our cool we maintain.
He can't share our feelings. This should be plain.
The emotions are all ours, no matter the strain.

Safe Harbor

Have a baby and you're committed for 22 years.
This was my philosophy as end of life nears.
I've rethought this with family extended.
And find my philosophy must be amended.
You really have a lifetime commitment to the young.
You are the safe harbor. A place they can come.
They in turn will provide a harbor for theirs.
Thus, we pass the responsibility on to our heirs.

Change

Some have called for change now and then.
I guess they're dissatisfied on how things have been.
But change for change sake may not be so great,
Since some widespread calamity may be our fate.
It could be wise to know for what we call,
And what we want changed either large or small.
Remember the saying, "Be careful what you call for."
The law of unforeseen consequences may get you more.

Masks

Masks have been the traditional way to hide.
People couldn't tell the real person inside.
This is fine for those who trick or treat
Or for party guests who fool those they meet.
Primitive people wanted to improve their odds,
While dancing and chanting, they fooled the Gods.
Modern people get used to wearing many a mask.
These are the invisible kind, if you need to ask.
One for church, one for the work place,

One for those at the club, or just in case,
One for school, one for a potential mate.
Impress that young lady on a first date.
There are so many, how do you keep track?
How can you remember just how to act?
At least when you're not out on the roam,
Lucky is the man who needs no mask at home.
My own personal way to act, a very good bet,
Be yourself. What you see is what you get.

Untitled Poems

We should remember the past as much as we can.
Preparing for the future is a pretty good plan,
But live in the present with total elan.

A great conversationalist in every way
Listens intently to what others say.
Ask a question but don't break the thought.
Keep comments short about answers sought.

A synonym for comprehend? It wasn't planned,
But we came up with the word understand?
I figure if you reverse it to stand under,
It shows how the usage is a blunder.

Don't take offence when none is meant,
Is the message that should be sent.
When someone does what's wrong in your view,
Maybe it's just ignorance. They haven't a clue.
So forget it. There's no insult to you.

Occasionally life will knock you around
And even kick you when you are down.
So whether you're a woman or a man,
Look for joy wherever you can.
Life may have dealt you a pretty bad blow,
But you're not the first one treated so.
So whether you're a girl or a boy.
Look all around you, and you'll find some joy.

I would if I could, but I can't so I won't
Are words you should live by but often don't.
Because no matter how much you rave and rant,
You still come back to the fact you can't.

I think I can, I think I can, requires some deeper thought.
There may be places where enthusiasm brings you naught.
In fact in an untenable situation you may be caught.
"I'll prevail or die trying," may be what you've bought.

"I'm awfully hot, Mom. I'm covered in sweat."
"Please say perspiration. You look pretty wet."
"I guess my perspiration glands are a wreck."
"Those are sweat glands to be correct."
Perspiration from perspiration glands is not right.
But sweat from sweat glands is impolite.

It's all about you?
What should I do.
You ought to agree,
It's all about me.

One life to live, that's all you get.
Making the most of it is your best bet.
Try to order things, so your body will last.
Slow down, enjoy, don't live so fast.

No good turn goes unpunished is the rule.
This truism you won't learn in school.
There's always hope you won't suffer from being kind.
Just be prepared and have this result in mind.
Take care. Don't go into the situation blind.

If I had a time machine, I wouldn't change the past,
Since I couldn't predict the outcome of such a die cast.
But I would like to travel back
To right some results of personal lack.
I didn't say thanks or I'm sorry. It's wrong.
This has plagued me for ever so long.

The king said to the philosopher of the court.
"Make up a nice saying, the appropriate sort,
That I could use with stranger and buddy."
"This too shall pass," was the result of the study.

When talking to a Navy man, don't make this slip,
Always refer to each of those floaters as a ship.
Except you'll manage to get his goat
If you call a submarine other than a boat.

Many of us in life want to do big things.
Maybe we seek fame and the wealth that it brings.
As far as fame goes, only the biggest names last.
Few are remembered as time flows past.
Wealth has the property of trickling away.
It was here in the past, but it's gone today.
I don't think either would mean much to me,
Compared to the importance of my family.

Sometimes you can feel agitated.
Maybe due to all the time you have waited.
Enough has happened to ruin your day.
However, nothing earth shaking, you could say.
So cheer up, you're not under a curse.
You know things could be a lot worse.
Put a smile on your face, the real kind.
It's all up to you, a good state of mind.

There's a difference between telling me what to do,
And asking with an added please or two.
Even the latter needs a pleasing tone,
This getting better results, should be widely known.

"You did me a favor. You helped me out.
How can I repay you and be a good scout?"
"You can't, but there is something you can do.
Pass it on when there's someone needing you."
This chain reaction would be nice if it grew.

Some folks, when enjoying themselves in their bliss,
Make the statement, "It doesn't get any better than this."
Of course, there's a fact that we can't deny,
On the down side of the hill, it'll still apply.

Why do people interrupt so much?
It seems they've lost the conversational touch.
They don't want to forget what they wish to say,
So the conversation is killed this way.

The most powerful sentence, I'll give you a clue.
It's also the shortest of which there are two.
The other's "I am," but the answer's "I do."

I have the impression, there should be a confession,
That our current recession, is really a depression.

The simplest sentence, the most punch per letter,
Is the pledge, "I do." There is none better.

To others, do you want to be more attractive?
Then keep your mind and body more active.

To make a handsome corpse, live fast and die young.
It may be romantic, but no praises will be sung.

Wisdom is the ability to make a decision that's right,
When only incomplete knowledge comes to light.

People who are fanatical about what they do
Have made life tough for all those they knew.

In our modern age of simple philosophy,
"Stuff happens." covers most any eventuality.

"Life's a bitch, then you die," seems lame to me.
Try to enjoy, "The best things in life are free."

Probably the best advice I can give to you,
Is from Hamlet, "To thine own self be true."

The lesson for losing weight is easy to learn.
Eat less calories than you burn.

4. Modern Life

Multi-tasking

Got more than one thing to do today?
Please don't do them while on your way.
Talking to friends on the mobile phone?
What the heck's wrong with being alone?
Sorry, but driving requires your full attention.
Consequences can follow too bad to mention.
No makeup, no shaving, no changing clothes.
Reading maps or the paper are all no-nos.
Think for a second about others around.
Your lack of care can put them in the ground.
For the rest of your life, do you want to feel bad,
Having killed a young mother or dad?
So use all your attention and stay alert,
And avoid the collision and the resulting hurt.

The Suburbs

After the war the GIs wanted to settle down.
With the quiet life and fresh air of a small town.
You could own a piece of land and your own house.
A great place to raise your kids with your spouse.
You wanted to rake the leaves and mow the lawn.
The yard work took little time and little brawn.
Gradually, the suburbs of the cities took form.
Living away from the crowding became the norm.
Now as the decades have passed us by,
I wonder about people and the reason why,
They choose to live outside of the city.
I see the crowded highways and have to take pity.
These folks hire others to trim, rake, and mow.
They would never paint and don't shovel snow.
The kids don't play outside enjoying the sun and air.
They're busy with electronic games and TV's blare.
They surf the net, they text, they cell.
They're in some kind of modern age spell.
I can't help thinking apartment living would be right,
Nothing to take care of, no traffic to fight.
More exercise walking to the subway or the bus.
Less stuff and no car about which to fuss.
I have this feeling, the solution is plain,
Live in the city. There's so much to gain.

Keeping Score

Kids learn early playing on sport teams,
You can win or lose no matter your dreams.
Well meaning parents and coaches don't keep score.
The kids, however, know what they're playing for.
They want to win. That's the reason for the game,
But the winner's place has but fleeting fame.
If they lose, they feel bad, but for a short bit.
They don't have life long damage or even a fit.
I think kids should learn how to lose and fail.
They'll learn it's not the end of the trail.
When you know how to fail, it's an easy pick up.
Then such travails of life will be just a hiccup.
After all, if at first you don't succeed,
Then try, try again will be your creed.

Your Day

Life can be tough when you're a teen.
Kids at that age can be so mean.
They seem to enjoy the apparent mirth
That results from their mocking your worth.
It may be easy for me to say.
Just don't accept their taunts in any way.
You know in the future you'll have your day.

Diets

In the old days we ate sugar and salt and saturated fat,
Refined flour, less fresh veggies and fruit. Stuff like that.
Now we have available food without the bad stuff.
With all that's fresh. For a good diet, this should be enough.
Yet people choose the worst from the past
Plus all the junk food for every repast.
No wonder the nutritionists are aghast.

Science, I'm Still Waiting

We may learn about science in articles and news.
Many of us don't understand the words that they use.
They build up the latest idea. They're really adorners.
How we'll get benefits that are just around the corners.
There are expected results from research on the stem cell.
They'll cure all sorts of things and make us well.
There's the promise of cures from the therapy of genes.
Small trials were disasters, if you know what I mean.
Nano technology will do wonders with tools so small,
There are university departments to discover it all.
The cosmologists rave over the theory of strings.
Think of the great progress this will bring.
Global warming will end if we control CO two.
All we have to do is develop some devices new.
Robots we are told will make great strides,
Though I have doubts about the benefits they'll provide.
All these new developments will make life great.
After a couple of decades, I wonder how long do we wait.
I think too many believe the projections they state.
If wishes were results, I wouldn't berate.

Modern Tools
Life gets physically easier. Is this good?
A bow saw was okay, now it's a chainsaw to cut fire wood.
A gas powered mower makes too much noise cutting grass.
For many years the no motor type would pass.
Now there's a snow blower, a shovel was fine.
Getting with the easy life, I've crossed the line.
Leaf blower, weed whacker, a power nail gun.
They make the work faster, but it's not so much fun.
Actually, it's not easier though the job's more quickly done.

Cells 1,2,3
Great for the kids when they need a ride.
Great for emergencies, maybe someone died.
Don't need to remind the kids to eat,
Or tell the hubby to buy a treat.
Their overuse by drivers makes me fearful.
If I could confront them, they'd get an earful.

Something you may see on a stone.
This is the a lesson, she had to be shown.
She drove while talking on her cell phone.

Cell phone,
Accident prone,
Had to be shown,
Life blown.

Exercise

My exercise regimen consists of moving weight.
I don't rest much, so I work at a steady rate.
This is aerobic with raised pulse and respiration.
It's somewhat like running but with moderation.
My technique should be the easiest exercise in town
Since most of the work is done while sitting down.

The Path Not Taken

No longer ask the question,
"Which road to take?"
No need for a digression,
With G.P.S., there's no mistake.
And so we'll miss
New discoveries made.
The unexpected bliss
Of an unknown glade.

The Junk Age

Maybe when archeologists dig through our remains,
They'll wonder about our apparent lack of brains.
It seems that as time progresses onward,
We choose the worst junk, and it's absurd.
We have the potential for a very good diet,
Yet we eat junk food. Why do we buy it?
The supermarket shelves are loaded with food, factory made.
We could prepare our own of a much better grade.
The very best music is available in hi-fi.
Yet we listen to crap that'll rattle the sky.
There are uncountable wonders about which we could learn.

Then we settle for junk entertainment. The best we spurn.
We fill our houses with all kinds of stuff.
Why do we have it? It's more than enough.
All the time we work so hard to get it.
The junk will control our lives if we let it.
Ancient civilizations declined, we can conclude,
When the stuff they made became more crude.
Are we aimed the same? Is it a certitude?

Handicapped Parking 1,2

The law says provide handicapped parking spaces.
There are scores at the home center type places.
They're never used at the local gym.
One blind guy attends, and someone drives him.
The hospital lot could use some more,
Though often the handicapped are dropped at the door.
For the truly handicapped, park in the fire lanes.
Changing this rule requires no brains.
Since most reserved spots are far from each store,
We'd give them a place closer to the door.

The handicapped when parking need a break,
So we provide spaces others shouldn't take.
However, there ought to be a limit of some kind.
Since often at some stores you'll find,
Only scofflaws or empty spaces, which I mind.

The Modern Age

I guess I'm just fifty years out of date.
Not wanting to join the modern age is my fate.
Others seem to take the internet okay.
For me there are better ways to spend my day.
I tell people, I have a limited number of hours.
I prefer to spend them smelling the flowers.
I don't want to be concerned with viruses and spam,
Worms and porno, email my brain would cram.
I have a computer. For typing it's great.
For googling I go elsewhere at a free rate.
The cell phone is another device I hate.
If I want to call, it's okay to wait.
People use them while driving with no excuse.
I have one, but it's only for emergency use.
People don't talk. Now they text.
I can't wait to see what's next.
Avoiding real conversation seems to be the goal.
Electronic gadgets help them to play this role.

Addictive Society

Our human society is addictive it seems.
New addictions for us show up by the reams.
In ancient times we had the big three,
Alcohol and tobacco and the eating spree.
I knew of gambling, heroin, and sex.
Though I knew no one who was so hexed.
Each of these addictions could wreck your life.
They certainly cause continuous family strife.

Now we have the benefits of our modern age,
Like the cornucopia of new drugs that are the rage.
Electronic devices steal our time.
TV was the first that propagated this crime.
The internet has its porno and face book.
Some spend all their time. They're really hooked.
Texting and its parent the cell,
Their overuse makes them devices from hell.
Some are addicted to a hobby or shopping.
Although they may try, there is no stopping.
Some addictions are what we're fanatical about.
They may not harm us, but they drive close ones out.
There is a solution if you never cheat.
Cold turkey can be used for all these to beat,
Except for the spree, we all have to eat.

Self Evident

Self evident for every device should be the motto.
Every time you meet a new one, you shouldn't go blotto.
Is it too much to ask for a visible on/off sign
With no need for a magnifier or bright light shine.
A plug-in socket with "power" would be nice.
You don't fool around. One trial should suffice.
Why the aversion to using English words plain?
Then old timers like me wouldn't go insane.
I've wrestled with my computer much too often.
Why is it necessary to have my poor brain soften?
All I ask for is a manual that's simple to read.
Trim all the bull and only say what you need.
For example: "To get the uncommon symbol list,

Double click with curser on "symbol"," the gist.

No need to consult with a youngster who knows.

Just simple descriptors, so you don't come to blows.

If I were in charge, before putting my gadget on sale,

I'd test it with a grandmother panel without fail.

Then the term "user friendly" would not be a lie.

Non-expert, real people would be able to get by.

User Friendly

When I hear "user friendly," I think, "watch out."

This usually means no descriptive material about,

And the "user" needs an expert "friend" no doubt.

PC's

I think an alternative to the PC by name

Would have us hooked up instead to a big main frame.

This would be tended by professional types,

And free the user from many gripes.

A keyboard and printer are what you would need.

Plus a terminal and a scanner which would run at high speed.

The procedure would be to throw the power switch.

In a few seconds, type your password with no glitch.

At this point all your personal type files,

And all software would be available by the piles.

Think of the advantages, nothing to install or buy.

No worry about viruses and other crap coming by.

The main frame can do everything the PC does now.

The user would have no need for computer knowhow.

No rebooting, no calls to experts and nerds.

We old folks and newbies would be attracted by herds.

Modern Education

Gee, the modern kids seem to know so much.

They can work all the electric gizmos and such.

Face book and texting and every electronic game,

Things we old folks can't even name.

And yet, there seems to be some bad news.

So many of them graduate without any clues,

About things I find really important to know.

The young haven't learned enough as they grow.

Most important is the ability to understand what you read,

All the written information that you really need.

You should be able to calculate a product or a sum,

So you don't get gypped by some financial bum.

You need to know how all of our governments work,

To be a good citizen and not a jerk.

History, science, geography to name some skills,

Economics, both personal and national may provide no thrills.

But together they make an educated person of you.

It's necessary in life when with school you're through.

Else wise, there's always low paying work to do,

Christmas Clubs

Remember the Christmas club. It was so quaint.

People actually saved money with no complaint.

You started in January saving for the holiday.

Then when December arrived, you had money to pay.

Divide the savings by the gifts to be bought,

And you found the average for those to be sought.

Now with no concern, we put it on the card.

No worry about overspending, not a word.

Just another way to run up a bill,

And overextend from a lack of will.

Finances in 1960

Forgive me if I return to the past.

Old timers, if they knew the future would be aghast.

I'd like to pick 1960 for a good year.

Then the USA's dominance was clear.

We produced two thirds of the world's manufactured goods.

The national debt was manageable as it stood.

Most families on one income could get by well enough.

They could buy a house, a car, and other stuff,

Afford medical insurance and the education of each child.

Life was pretty good, with spending, nobody went wild.

We earned a down payment with just six month's pay.

How long does it take in the current day?

Economists said maybe we should cut the work week,

Since productivity in no way had hit its peak.

We'd need less workers to man each plant and mill.

There would be too many, with limited jobs to fill.

So we did the opposite by exporting many a job.
The work for Americans was what was robbed.
Let's jump forward to the modern day.
Does anyone understand what happened along the way?
If you want to buy some item that's American made,
You may find nothing. It's all from foreign trade.
Two incomes are needed, a house to buy,
Medical and education costs will make you cry
What the heck happened? I can't figure, no matter how I try.

The Elite

No wonder the elite of the northeast and west coast
Are so strongly disliked and more so than most.
They've pushed policies that are causing the country's ruin.
Many of us wonder just what they are doin'.
The worst is the export of technology and jobs.
Somehow they don't care about the poor people they rob.
Tell a sixty year old man he can retrain for a new field.
Maybe his wounds, by some service sector job, will be healed
His town will die. All who can move will do so.
Though they can't sell their houses, another blow.
Let's face it. We now have the survival of the most fit.
These are the wealthy. The rest are the ones who get hit.
The motto of the day is, "Well tough____."

Enough Yet

The forty something man had a cardiac event.

Afterward, to a rehab program he was sent.

They gave him a list of changes in life style

Which wouldn't take much time. This made him smile.

However, there was one exception, the need to walk

Or to exercise on a treadmill. He began to balk.

"My minimum work day is ten hours long. So when?

Our boss drives us. We have to be supermen."

Then he thought of all the activities that take time.

Those required of a good person in his prime.

Be a good citizen, volunteer, take a course,

Read the paper, get news from the best source.

Fix what's broken, take care of the yard.

Help the kids with homework if it's too hard.

Be a scout leader and coach the kids' teams.

Help your friends and neighbors, as hard as it seems.

Have a hobby, and to lift your life,

Make sure you take time to love your wife.

Since there's no way in hell he'll have any time free,

This busy guy seems to have choices three.

Give up sleep, approach his boss with a plea,

Or say the hell with it all and watch TV.

Our Age

Food-gunk.

Music- punk.

Entertainment- stunk.

Gadgets- junk.

Chill It

Much I don't like about the modern world.
When I dwell on it, my lunch is hurled.
Said another way, things make me ill.
Stop, I want to get off. I've had my fill.
Only kidding. I guess I should just chill.

Wonder

Sometimes I wonder about some of the young.
When they come in contact, they seem so glum.
Perhaps they're afraid of a social faux pas,
So they keep a neutral face, sort of blah.
My advice is, it's okay to smile and say, "Hi."
For the big world, this will help you get by.
The aspect of cheerfulness is the reason why.

Wants

You want that thing. You want it now.
You don't care the cost. You don't ask how.
Even if it's more than your finances allow.

5. Society's Stupidities

Innocence

Scene 1

At the wedding, Johnny bears the rings.

Five year old Mary, each flower petal flings.

So serious and steady they walk the aisle.

Each of the guests watches the two with a smile.

At the reception Johnny sneaks a kiss.

The photographer catches this moment of bliss.

How cute they are, how sweet.

For all who see, it's such a treat.

Scene 2

Johnny sees Mary during the school day.

He plants a kiss. He thinks it's okay.

He sees adults show affection this way.

But unfortunately, the purists have their say.

Johnny, age five, is sent for detention.

To stop harassment, you need intervention.

Calling mom in, should get his attention.

Making him an example is their intention.

Guns

The rules say zero tolerance concerning the gun.
Little boys can shoot while having their fun.
At home a kid can have pistols, water or cap.
He can play cops and robbers. There is no flap.
A kid will buy rifles at any toy store.
He's exposed to violence, on TV there's more.
Yet if by chance, he takes a toy to school,
He'll risk being severely punished by some fool.
Is there any justification for being so cruel?

Do It

The law says do it, so we do it.
Sometimes though, we ought to rue it.
We have blanket rules, we must obey.
Common sense is lost along the way.

Weapons

I made each child weapons of war.
Of this I could hardly do more.
Rifle, dagger, pistol, and sword,
All cut out from a soft pine board.
Into psychos, did they grow?
They're all gentle people, this I know.

Legal Errors 1,2

Because of an error, the perp goes free.
More exposed to terror, another crime spree.
Is it reasonable to us, the peaceful ones?
We'll just sit there and cuss, the stupidity stuns.

A cop makes a mistake, the criminal goes free.
I'm not sure about you, it seems stupid to me.
If the cop breaks the law, charge him with a crime.
For mistakes in procedure, dock his pay for some time.
Maybe the jury should make any ruling.
They'd do better than the judge, no fooling.

No Touching

The poor teacher, what should she do?
The rules are set, everything is so new.
She can't touch a child, no matter the need.
So push him away, the rules she must heed.
Sometimes they just need a hug or a touch.
With all the world's problems, it's not so much.

New Rules

Common sense has gone by the board.
Some rules and decisions have me floored.
A water pistol is classed with an Uzi.
A jackknife makes some people feel woozy.
A harmless smooch by a five year old,
Results in a school suspension I'm told.
Sexual predators, little boys are not.
To think they'd spray bullets is simply rot.
Tell them what's acceptable in school.
Please let old time common sense rule.

Shopping 1,2,3

Traditionally, fresh food was available to touch.
The shopper could select each item and how much.
Now there's less freedom in the choices you make.
Often, the quantity wrapped is what you must take.
However, this method has a great advantage for you.
The food isn't touched by each shopper passing through.
I once saw a lady pick up every lettuce head,
Then didn't buy any, getting something else instead.
Maybe if people want to squeeze veggies and fruit,
Wearing throw any plastic gloves would suit.

Going through the supermarket isn't a race.
So don't block others trying to pass your place.
On the left some folks will park their cart,
While examining the right. It's not very smart.
Parking the cart at an angle is worse.
This blocks the way and is so perverse.
Please restrict yourself to half the aisle.
Then other shoppers will give you a smile.

To empty your cart at the checkout lane,
Stand next to the belt and lessen back pain.
No reaching down deep or across the cart.
To save your back, you should be smart.
Use both hands from the very start.

The Idiots Have Taken Over

Maybe we've always had idiots around,
But it seems to me they're gaining ground.
The latest problem they've created for us
Is punishing kids by making a big fuss,
For the tiniest infraction of a stupid rule.
We can't have "dangerous " things in school.
I expect the schools should also clean up their act,
By removing everything that could be used in an attack.
Therefore, no scissors in class, in the kitchen no knives,
No ball bats, no string for choking out lives.
Nothing with points, no sharp pencil or pen.
Better get rid of all glass if you can.
Nothing that could be thrown, like a book.
You can find "dangerous" stuff wherever you look.
There are many "dangerous" objects, like all the tools,
That could hurt some kid in our schools.
Think of all kids when you make up your rules.

Kids Aren't Criminals

The worse things I've seen little kids do
Is throwing a toy or a hard soled shoe.
They're known to knock you with their heads,
Or give a bite which most moms dread.
They don't stab with a jackknife or cutting tool.
They don't spray bullets at classmates in school.
Any attack they make is spontaneous for sure.
They don't plan an attack. They're not that mature.

No Letters

Millennia ago our ancestors developed the letter.
Compared to the hieroglyph, they certainly are better.
We don't have to rely on pictures of things
With the uncertainty that this system brings.
Now the written word is going out of style.
The latest cells have symbols by the pile.
Cars have many a warning light instead of a dial.
I like words like temp, gas, and oil
Instead of some picture which makes my blood boil.

Judgment

A cop shoots a suspect on a dark street.
His reaction results from a moment of heat.
He had to act or not without hesitation.
He'll be judged by people in quiet deliberation.

Toy Guns

No toy guns in the house, peace will rein.
But an index finger works, so what did you gain.

6. Religion and Good Deeds

The Next Step

I have entered the twilight of my years.
I know not when, though the end is near.
Relatives and friends say, "Don't talk that way,"
But they know there'll be a final day.
I tell them, they should not feel bad for me,
Since I've had the greatest life there could be.
What will come next, none of us knows.
We all hope the best as life slows.
Is there a heaven where only the most pious go,
And the remainder spend eternity in fires below?
I can't picture a loving God casting aside
All those who the rules did not wholly abide.
Whatever comes, I know what I'd like to see.
First a meeting with those who passed before me.
Some to say thanks, some to say I'm sorry.
These simple gestures often were dilatory.
I'd like to find how things turned out.
Did the grand kids find good spouses without doubt?
Did our young and all those coming after them
Have contented and meaningful lives in tandem?
The world is facing many problems, it's true.
Would I see that intelligence solved many or few?

Will mankind survive beyond this age,
Or will we revert to a primitive stage?
Maybe we'll just cease to exist when we die.
Maybe heaven and hell are human inventions is why.
We can't imagine the world when we're not here.
Do our beliefs create an afterlife from this fear?

Charities

I've decided to limit each charitable gift.
There are so many, they need a sift.
Many pay their top people too much I'd say.
They use the argument, "To get top people you need to pay."
Well forget my contribution. I won't donate a cent
To any organization where money is so spent.
I'll list some if I may including the Boy Scouts.
The United Way and the Red Cross. Do I hear any shouts?
How about any hospital or private school.
Some are money pits. I won't be a fool.
How many contributions for the salaries at the top?
Excessive salaries for them has to stop.
Think logically. Does a CEO really want to help fill a need
When his interest is driven entirely by greed?

Thanks

I never said thanks to my Mom and Dad.
They were the best that anyone has had.
They taught me without teaching the living rules.
Things that somehow aren't taught in schools.
By example they taught me to be kind, honest, and fair,
And how to help when I can, and how to share.

How to be frugal, how to work hard,

When to be open and when to be on guard.

But more important than anything listed above.

How to be both a receiver and a giver of love.

I know I never said the words when I could,

But I feel them every day as I know I should.

Forgiveness

There's no commandment that says, "Thou shalt forgive."

Though it should be a rule by which you live.

Forgiving a hurt which eats at your guts.

Might just keep you from going nuts.

For a healthy body and mind you need to live

By taking this advice, "Do your best to forgive."

Lullaby

Go to sleep little man. It's getting late.

We don't want to make the sandman wait.

Tomorrow you and I will play again.

We'll have a great time, just us men.

When you grow up, you'll be big and strong.

Time flies by. It won't take very long.

Now a prayer for the close of day.

God protect you. Keep serious hurt away.

In Need

The dinner was there for the old or those in need.

Most of us contributed a donation, a good deed.

A middle age lady stared to cry.

Passing people might wonder why.

Her husband or boyfriend tried to console.
No one would ask her to bare her soul.
I can imagine the cause of her sorrow.
Maybe job loss or bankruptcy was due tomorrow.
She felt a loss of stature eating with the old,
Which she shouldn't, if I may be so bold.
One day she'll be serving when the future unfolds.

Act of Faith

The religious and non-religious among us,
Both practice acts of faith without fuss.
In fact they don't even think about this,
And blindly charge ahead with utter bliss.
Consider the puddle on a city street.
Is it an inch deep or a tire blowing pothole you'll meet?
When you bring fresh produce home or eat out,
Do you have the faintest idea or the slightest doubt
Concerning its cleanliness and who touched it?
Crop picker, preparer, fellow shopper or twit.
Who knows what pathogen you may ingest.
Each bite is an act of faith I guess.

Fish Story

The bible says, feed me a fish, you feed me today.
If you teach me to fish, you feed me always.
Our welfare laws should keep this in mind
When helping the able bodied, you'd be more kind
By helping self sufficiency. The result's better you'll find.

Doers of Good

Doer of good, doer of good,
I would help you if I could,
But your project may have no effect.
Though that's not your reason I expect.
You want to feel good, hence your hard work,
And I have other causes I cannot shirk.

The Gift

A knock on the door, "Here's a gift for you."
"There must be some mistake. We're not needy."
"But please take it." The man has much to do,
And wants to feel good. I shouldn't be greedy.
The conundrum here, take it so he feels good,
Or refuse it as I know I should.

Prejudice

Ah, those who are prejudiced and don't know it,
Can make hateful statements that certainly show it.
When I hear a general statement, to whit,
"Women are such bad drivers," it gives me a fit.
"Engineers are so one dimensional, they're unaware
Of the arts, languages, and beauty out there."
I've heard people, those among the elite,
Who judge others who live on the wrong street.
If they don't wear clothes that are in style,
Then you can't see their company is worth your while.
My car is newer and more expensive than yours.
Therefore, I'm better. Any equality we have blurs.
My house is bigger, yours is a trailer.

Thus, you must be trash, one of life's failures.
The same people would never generalize about Blacks.
Hispanics and Asians would not suffer attacks.
For professing Christians or the conservative types
Be sure you belittle them and those of their stripes.
What gets me most are those preaching diversity and love,
When they look down on the lower casts from their perches above.

Secrets

Did you ever know a secret told to you or not,
And kept it year in, year out whatever your lot?
An old friend didn't want his secret known.
He lived with his dad in a tar paper home.
I swore to myself, I would never reveal
Except to my wife who has a mind she can seal.
I only told her 50 years after the fact.
For all that time there was no need for a pact.
We've kept other secrets for a full life long.
Make a pledge to yourself. It can't be wrong.
Keep secrets buried where they belong.

Seven

The Pharaoh told Joseph about a dream.

He wondered just what it could mean.

It seems that seven fat cows were eaten by seven lean.

We're aware of Joseph's interpretation,

About the fat and lean of seven years duration.

The Pharaoh paid attention to Joe's deliberation.

We've had more than seven times seven to prepare

For the economic crisis we all will share.

Somehow the powerful among us don't care.

Two Letters

Can you make a short sentence with just two letters?

Would this interest those of you who are betters?

Here's a clue that you may have heard.

One's a vowel that's also a word.

Don't bet unless ancient history you know.

It reads the same both to and fro.

Give up? The Pharaoh said about his sib.

I've found she's godly. I will not fib.

Sis is Isis.

Best Friend

Poor Adam by himself was kind of blue,

So God said, "I'll do something for you."

And he created Eve to share the earth.

He thought again with a bit of mirth,

And created the dog to be man's best friend.

He gave him a name changing front to end.

God has a sense of humor, I'd contend.

A Good Deed

One of the easiest ways to do a good deed,
Is to give blood. This fills a big need.
You'll never know to whom you give.
Just know you helped someone to live.
Of your time, it takes but an hour.
It hardly hurts, no need for valor.
While you're giving blood, you're lying down,
The easiest good turn anywhere in town.

A Test

How decent are you? Here's a test.
Do you treat those well you've never met?
If you're kind to them, you'll be blest,
And humanity will be in your debt.
Not only should you be kind to me,
But also to all those you'll never see.
All religions on this ought to agree.

Equality

We're all equal in God's eye I'm told,
And under man's law too, the courts uphold.
But there are so many who consider themselves better.
Me thinks their heads and hearts are in a fetter.

7. Mother Nature

Signs of Spring

We all know signs of Spring. In a word
Most notice the song of the returning bird.
They get here early. They don't want to be late
In claiming territory and attracting a mate.
They're here, but there are no bugs to eat.
Maybe last year's seeds provide a treat.
Most people may look for forsythia and crocus,
But the sign of thawed ground should be our focus.
There is a sign mentioned by none.
It's the presence of earthworm poop, no pun.
When the ground is thawed, a certain sign,
The worms can burrow upward, and the robins dine.
New plant growth follows from thawed ground.
Soon bugs and caterpillars can be found.

Watching

We've been observing birds for many a year.
Their antics and singing have given us cheer.
When we added our screened porch to the house's side,
We changed from the plan to make it less wide.
This was to save a pine tree with branches low.
It gave shade. It needed room to grow.
During the warm weather, we ate dinner there.

Without the bugs these were picnics with no care.
One year a pair of blue jays built a nest
Right next to the screen. Why be our guest.
We didn't use the porch for several weeks.
Though through the kitchen window we could peek.
The nest was constructed of grass and sticks.
I don't know how it stayed together with this mix.
Mom or maybe dad, we couldn't tell them apart,
Carefully sat on four eggs from the very start.
They chased scavenging crows after sounding the alarm.
They wouldn't let their precious eggs come to harm.
Once Grandma heard that raucous alarm cry.
She threw a rock and made the crows fly.
The real work began when the young were hatched.
One would sit. The other brought the insect catch.
Then both parents would search and bring food.
About eating, the young were always in the mood.
What good parents, four fledged from four eggs.
After leaving the nest, the young would still beg.
We watched full size jays fluttering their wings.
Please bring food, like babies they'd sing.
We were happy for the birds when they left the nest.
We could use our porch again for dinner and rest.

New Disease

Mother nature has provided diseases by the score.
I counted up almost thirty. There are more.
These were all around fifty years ago,
And all are pathogen caused, I know.

This doesn't include cancer or strokes and the like.
There are dozens more ways your body can strike.
Now in the last few decades what's new.
I counted fourteen, and I know we're not through.
Mother nature has more in store than AIDS and flu.
Will we survive the resistant diseases' brew?
We should push for great effort to fight
With research on possible treatments of this blight.

Survival

How did the human race survive over the ages
With the big three P's confronting us at all stages?
I'll refresh your memory if you don't know.
Predators, parasites, and pestilence each gave its blow.
Tooth and claw certainly killed enough in the early day.
Think how you'd feel seeing your child snatched away.
Team work and the invention of the weapon and tool,
Essentially took care of the predators most cruel.
Parasites have been conquered it seems,
Unless you live in a poor society that teems.
Pestilence, ever changing will always be with us.
More than a dozen new ones, bacteria and virus,
Have appeared to plague us in the last few decades.
Their ability to mutate and propagate never fades.
If the three P's weren't enough to make life hell,
We can starve, freeze, or die in child birth as well.
Man, of course, will always find a way.
We kill each other in war even to this day.

In modern times, we find our bodies fail.
We have dozens of maladies to make us ail.
We may die quickly by heart attack or stroke,
Or have lingering agony before we croak.
In any case, it's surprising mankind's still here.
I guess optimism and faith give us cheer.

Climate Change
CO2 is bad, but methane is worse.
This is what's called a human flatus curse.
Cut its production by dietary means.
That's why we take the pledge of no beans.

King Of Beasts
The lion's called the king of beasts on land.
I'd guess the sperm whale has the title beyond the sand.
Perhaps the harpy eagle owns the sky,
And one of the crocs is king where rivers lie
(Except where hippos challenge for those domains.)
But hold on. Maybe man's the real king who reigns.
All these are wrong, I have to claim,
Since each one has pestilence that'll kill or maim.
It seems that man, the highest form of life
Has maladies that are the most rife.
Disease and parasites will always cause us woe.
Is there really a king? I'd have to say no.

Survival Of the Fittest

One point of evolutionary theory is the most fit
Survive and procreate as luck or strength would permit.
What does most fit mean in a special way?
Bigger, tougher or better armed, you could say.
Can the most fit prevail against the rest of its kind
And protect its offspring if it is of mind?
Is being most able mean avoiding being a meal?
Is the ability to find food part of the deal?
These properties of course are not the case,
Since surviving disease and parasites, we all must face.
Mother Nature doesn't care how we make out,
And has provided for our demise no doubt.
I'd guess luck is what survival is all about.

Nature's Decree

For every species Mother Nature has a decree.
Each will suffer and die from one of three.
First the predators will limit numbers.
Then disease your health encumbers.
Finally, if your kind increases enough,
Lack of food, your life will snuff.
For the survival of individuals, Mother Nature doesn't care.
Even entire species she deems not to spare.
Long time species survival seems to be quite rare.

Untitled Poems

The predators want to eat you up.
Parasites and pests on your blood will sup.
What's the worst, I don't know which?
I do know Mother Nature is a bitch.

With pathogens both left and right,
It's an act of faith with every bite.

It's no exaggeration that we need more preparation,
To counter the situation of disease proliferation.

A sure sign that the ground is thawed,
The presence of earthworm poop. I knew you'd be awed.

8. The Male Female Thing

Advice to a Lady

The young lady at work seemed rather blue.
We talked a bit. She didn't actually ask me what to do.
She was somewhat stocky. You could describe her as plain,
But she was sweet and kind. I knew she had a brain.
She wanted to meet a guy, someone to share her life.
A career wasn't enough. She wanted to be a mother and wife.
I was no expert on the matter, but I had a plan.
I said she needed to show interest to attract a man.
Way back a lady would drop a hanky near a guy.
He'd rush to pick it up, no matter if he were shy.
She showed interest in this simple way,
And this technique still works to this day.
Maybe a girl will push a boy while they play.
No need to use words, the message to convey.
Drop a stack of books. Look helpless with the mess.
If he's any kind of gentleman, he'll help, I'd guess.
It's okay to drop your lunch or coffee on his lap.
If he gets upset, you can cry for being a sap.
Whatever you do, you've attracted his attention.
Maybe it doesn't matter if he knows your intention.
Perhaps a modern lady would think this is dumb,

A rather dishonest way to attract some male bum.
All I know is that a few months later,
An engagement ring appeared. What could be greater?
They married, had kids, and are together to this day.
Apparently, with my advice, she did it the right way.
All is fair in love and war, they could say.

Alone

A science fiction story described an alien race.
Their society was connected, everyone in the place.
Each could feel all others' joy and pain.
It was somehow due to the connection of each brain.
The aliens couldn't understand how we got by
With no real interaction, we should die.
When one alien cut off all connection with his kind,
He immediately and literally lost his mind.
I've often thought that we are terribly alone.
When they cut the cord, we are on our own.
We seek friendship and closeness for a full life.
The best we can do is the love between man and wife.
Even then we may think we know the other one.
It's only a tiny part, when all is said and done.
No matter what, we just can't feel what another feels,
But even then, it's the best of all deals.

Asking Directions

About men, women have this ancient objection.
When apparently lost, men just won't ask directions.
Women will take the opposite sway.
Figuring any fool they meet will know the way.

Toilets

All you men, if you don't want to be beat,

Make sure you leave down that toilet seat.

I know this is a widespread problem of our times.

The violators are guilty of serious crimes.

However, if you don't lift the seat while using,

You're sure to get wacked and a bruising.

To live a peaceful life, men should do their bit,

So the gals can avoid looking before they sit.

My wife's the exception, we have three boys.

She always checked first, also to retrieve any toys.

Tandem

Life is better lived in tandem.

Much better than sex at random.

You have a lover and friend in one.

Life this way is a lot more fun.

You can be yourself, no need to act.

A good way to live, and that's a fact.

Failures

It takes a lot of looking, so it seems.

Most of the young have a perfect mate in their dreams.

That perfect someone who will always love us.

Of course, it should be mutual. That's the plus.

However, we should know, there are no princesses ideal,

And the fairy tale Prince Charming isn't real.

We should look for who would be a good mate.

Hopefully, we'll find the one before it's too late.

The advice on this ought to be clear.

Of love's failures, you should have no fear.

Only one success in love is all you need.

If you make it permanent by word and deed.

Be Definite

"Be definite," the wife would always say.

She wants her big strong man to be that way.

We're going out to eat. She says, "You pick."

I innocently don't think this really is a trick.

Wrong answer when I say, "I don't really care."

She says, "You should pick, and we'll go there."

So I say, "Okay, lets go to A." Wrong again.

"I'd really prefer B," she states (what's wrong with men?)

She wants me to decide so she can decide her way.

Originally, I didn't have the skill for the game we play,

But I have learned and remain happy to this day.

The Games Afoot

I'm not sure that the young know love's a game.

Though the rules for the guys and gals aren't the same.

If the participants are smart, they'll play by the rules.

Though they sometimes may feel like fools.

You may ask, "What are these rules to obey?"

I'm not telling. The fun's learning along the way.

One thing you should do from the very start,

Don't try to act. Be true to your heart.

Love and Marriage

In the time well before the modern day

The young grew up knowing their way.

There was an excepted order of things in life.

Get educated, get a decent job, while looking for a wife.

We got married, and soon had a kid.

We saved up, buying a house was what we did.

The wife stayed home to be a full time mother.

Of all possible lives, we wanted no other.

Now the young want to wait until later.

The lack of responsibility has a pull that's greater.

The maturity that we had, they apparently lack.

Perhaps the storied Peter Pan phenomena is back.

They just don't want to grow up it seems.

Maybe they have another set of dreams.

Beaters

There are some males who have no sense.

Feeling they can own someone, is their offense.

Having full control is what owning means here.

They mix their definitions of love and fear.

To keep control of their kith and kin,

They have to bully them by fist or din.

They can't check their anger, so they say,

But this is bull. I'll explain if I may.

A husky man in reasonable shape, I know.

Could kill a woman or child with one blow.

On loss of control, don't let them fool you.

They know exactly what they do.

Note this fact that's always true.

They'll never change since their brain's askew.

Joining

When you're joined together, you make the splice,

At the ceremony where they throw the rice.

Some would say you pay the price

Of having chanced the toss of dice.

What you have is the life of spice.

The Chase

There's the old game of which modern folks know naught.

Therefore, I'll paraphrase. Thus, you'll be taught.

He chased the young lady until he was caught.

Choices
Marry a fanatic, and you have choices three.
Join in the activity and show some glee,
Ignore the activity and choose what you want to be,
Or go your own way and choose to be free.

Strife
How will we ever stop world strife,
When we have a man who'll beat his wife?

Untitled Poems
Why is it that a women will take two chairs?
One's for her purse, The other for her derriere.
If someone is standing near by, she doesn't care.

To avoid crashing into the deep
Just look before you leap.
To avoid having a tizzy fit
Just look before you sit.

Women usually have to carry a purse.
Not having some item would be a curse.

One hundred failures, is this the worst?
No, not trying your best on the hundred and first.

"Cold hands, warm heart," is what lovers used to say.
"Cold feet, hot pants," is for the modern day.

Whether they're men or mice
Love is the life of spice.

9. College

College Donations

We get begging letters from the Old State U.

Plus other schools, there are more than a few.

We have a connection with at least eight more.

They all would like support. They make me sore.

When I distribute my fortune most great.

None will get anything on that prestigious date.

I shall list some reasons that come to mind.

Here are a few, and I may be too kind.

Excessive cost, with inflation, it's out of line.

Too much pay for presidents and coaches, a bad sign.

For sports programs, too much cost.

The emphasis on academics has been lost.

No hint of requiring kids to obey the law.

When there is date rape, this is the last straw.

They turn away from drunkenness, cheating, and drug use,

Allowing kids to harm themselves is a type of abuse.

Generally, the requirements are lax, the school year short,

The education in many cases is worthless I can report.

For any money I spend on the educational front,

I'll give to my grand kids, and I mean to be blunt.

To Do Good

Kids are taught about doing good in life.

There are problems we face including world strife.

It's nice to feel you ought to do your part.

To fix any problem, one needs to be smart.

However, when choosing what subjects to learn,

Taking the soft majors is a path you should spurn.

You'll never solve anything unless you have knowledge.

You should work on your courses while in college.

Take engineering or hard science and learn hard stuff.

Then to make a contribution, you'll know enough.

Off to College

Going off to college, I had very little stuff.

One suitcase for my clothes was quite enough.

A goose neck lamp, a wastebasket, a clock,

Linens, bathroom stuff, a dictionary, a combo lock,

All fit in my car's trunk with space to spare.

No need for my parents to drive me there.

Now kids have to be driven with a trailer load.

To get all their stuff to their new abode.

They need all that electronic stuff to survive at school.

A microwave and a frig makes food hot or cool.

Unfortunately, they have the same dorm place.

How can they cram everything in that small space?

The Rules

In loco parentis was the rule of the day.
Colleges acted like parents in an important way.
Students were expected to obey the laws of the land.
Illegal behavior was squelched out of hand.
No boys in the girl's dorm, nor girls in the boy's.
Just like home rules, that each parent employs.
No drugs tolerated, nor any hard booze.
Being suspended from school was the bad news.
Now parents pay fortunes to send their kids to school,
Where the kids can destroy themselves with the lack of rules.

The College Mess

College costs are unbelievable now.
They've exceeded what normal inflation would allow.
Tuition was four hundred, fifty years ago.
Now forty thousand gives parents a blow.
Then, a kid could earn it summers, it's clear.
Now he's lucky if his dad earns that in a year.
Couple this with a school year that's short,
And kids taking gut courses like a sport.
Mark inflation means kids study much less.
Partying is why they go to school I guess.
Students and their parents should know it's a mess.

Helping

If you want to help out some poor guy,
Then know what you're doing and here's why.
Being stupid won't do, no matter how hard you try.
Your mistakes could cause someone to die.

Wisdom

A wise professor's advice tried and true,
In life find what you'd love to do,
Then find someone who'll gladly pay you.

10. Politics and Wealth

Hypocrisy Reigns

There's been a move to make us all green.
Conserve all things, your plate you should clean.
Don't waste energy, turn off the lights.
Lower the thermostat on cold winter nights.
Don't own a big gas guzzling car,
And whatever you drive, don't go very far.
We old timers were raised this way.
We know how to conserve from our earliest days.
But we are preached at by people of note.
They tell us all this. They get my goat.
In particular the earth is warming, warns Al Gore.
The carbon dioxide we emit is at its core.
Yet Big Al lives in a mansion, quite large
With lights burning too much I can charge.
I will bet he doesn't drive any tiny car.
He probably generates more CO2 by far
Than several poor or middle class families do.
Should people pay attention, me and you?
The Nobel Committee gave him their Peace Prize.
I can't understand. He's a hypocrite in my eyes.
And is there anything worse than this?
In addition, his arrogance none can miss.
It's bad enough when this hypocrite tells us what to do.
When he's arrogant about it, I say screw you.

Windmills

One way to eliminate CO_2 is to use wind power.
This renewable resource is from turbine towers.
The energy is free. The equipment is the cost,
And transmission means some energy is lost.
Lets try it out. Nantucket Sound seems right.
But there's a problem. They'd be in the wealthy's sight.
Can't have them in their front yard. Oh no!
Put them where the lesser people go.
Thus, the hypocrites strike as they often do.
They want green energy. Just not within their view.

Immigrants

From wealth and privilege, none of them fled.
They wanted a better life, it's often been said.
Religious freedom or the opportunity to take a chance.
No guarantee in this perceived land of abundance.
The earlier the pilgrimage, the harder the trip,
Months at sea on a sailing ship.
If they survived the crossing, what did they face?
A land that could be a rather hostile place.
It was easier for those who came later.
They surely felt blest by their creator.
There is no doubt, they were brave and tough.
In modern parlance, they had the right stuff.
Whatever the group, they wanted to stay,
And adopt the new country, its language and ways.
For the latest groups, is it still true?
Are they willing to adopt the red, white, and blue,
And all it stands for to me and to you?

Politics

A political observation made by my son,
Considers philosophy when all's said and done.
Conservatives feel you should take care of your own,
While liberals feel it's the government's job alone.

Forebears

About our forebears, we must be frank.
None fled wealth, privilege, or rank.
For this great land, their God they thank.

Free Talk

It's been a constant amazement to me
That a notable person will go on a verbal spree.
You should know that a careless midday remark
Will make the news before it gets dark.
With ten thousand reporters wanting to make a name,
They'll make sure for each booboo you'll get the blame.
And yet you spout. It's an embarrassment in the least
While the media has its frenzied feast.

Interpretation

Interpreting the constitution shouldn't take much smarts.
"Congress shall make no law," the first amendment starts
"...abridging the freedom of speech or of the press..."
Somehow freedom of expression seems to be an excess.
It's not okay to express yourself with exposure in the nude,
Though it's okay to be noisily and publicly crude.
It's legal for you to burn a flag in a public place.

If I throw water, guess who the cops will chase.
If you display a cross in a beaker of pee,
My tipping it over would be a crime you see.
It depends on who's expressing themselves here.
The radical person or the one who holds the symbol dear.
If you hate the flag and cross, and all they stand for,
Then find a better place. I'll show you the door.

Radicals

When the young radicals want to riot and shout,
They claim freedom of speech is what it's about.
When someone they disagree with wants to be heard,
They yell and scream so none can hear a word.
They reserve for themselves our freedom of speech.
Any opposing view should be kept out of reach.
Such feelings are common in our schools for the elite.
This is reason enough to prefer the man in the street.

Separation

Some radicals hate the military and the cop.
With their vehemence, they know not when to stop.
Hating some politician and his policies isn't the same
As hating these people, since they're not to blame.
Your local policeman has nothing to do with this.
Why not treat him courteously? He doesn't need the dis'.
For God's sake, they're not the radical's enemy here.
Just think for a second and this ought to be clear.
However,

I've often wondered when a radical is robbed with a gun,
Or after some other calamity, where does he run?
Does he call a friend to come help him out?
Would he trust the cops or have some doubt?
Maybe we should separate people into two groups.
The haters get no aid from the cops or the troops.

Assassins

Modern rulers of the world should take care.
There's a tremendous number of crazies out there.
If an assassin is willing to die trying to kill,
It's almost impossible to thwart his will.
It's not necessary to slap a back or shake a hand
While openly wandering about the land.
For all our sakes, take the caution we demand.

CEO Pay

The top man usually gets the big buck.
He deserves this to guarantee the company's luck.
No one really objects as long as he does his job,
Though even in normal times, there's the question," Did he rob?"
"Our company is better than yours," is the claim.
"We pay our CEO more." It's the one up game.
Would you want your company's low paid guy
Discussing business with all the big fry?
When we get the alternate scenario, he fails.
At this time the company he has led, derails.
One would expect the big CEO would be a man,
And refuse any pay, and all bonuses he'd ban.

No extenuating circumstances, the buck stops here.
It's his job to keep the company healthy, to steer.
And yet we have really big shots accepting big pay
When their company flounders from errors and moral decay.
Meanwhile the workers at the bottom of the pile,
Accept their layoffs. They bear it and smile.
Just think, every million dollar bonus gift
Would provide a hundred folks with a ten grand lift.

Wealthy

I don't mind the wealthy if their money is earned.
Inherited wealth means life's lessons weren't learned.
The earner may know how it is to be poor.
The other wealthy would never know for sure.

Big Wealth

Big money, big appetite, big house, big car,
You flaunt it, so people will know who you are.
A lot of big service is needed for big stuff.
Part time cleaners and gardeners are not enough.
You hire a nanny since mom's too busy.
The need for professional help makes me dizzy.
Since the wealthy, at heart, are pretty cheap,
They find paying a decent wage is much too steep.
Thus, they hire aliens at the lowest wage.
"They get what they pay for," said a wise old sage.

Two Classes

When our big shots, their wealth they amass,
They seem to be creating an upper and lower class.
The lower are those who cater to each need.
Having personal servants is a result of their greed.
Our nation was not meant for a two class society.
The thought of this gives me great anxiety.
My personal goal is to take care of my own stuff.
The need to hire, means I've got more than enough.

The Goal

An unstated liberal refrain,
You should lose, so he can gain
Don't expect me to share the pain.
Our plan is to get you to help him.
This is our goal and not a whim,
Along the way your rights we'll trim.

Untitled Poems

Do what I say and not what I do,
The hypocrite implies. Should we take his cue?
Maybe we should forget what he's said,
And do what he does instead.

If you think raising taxes would be more fair,
Remember, you can always pay more than your share.
Putting money where your mouth is, says you care.

The wealthy don't need to work.
Some poor choose to shirk.
Others labor because of each perk.
If none work, disaster will lurk.

The non-working poor and the wealthy are in league.
They want to eliminate the middle class through intrigue,
And the latter may fall from working fatigue.

The economy benefits from a certain amount of greed.
People work extra hard to satisfy some need.
When greed is extreme and gets out of hand,
It can cause a collapse of proportions grand.

A criminal steals, he's not too bright.
The self centered CEO thinks it's his right.

11. Cars

Inspection
My lifelong agony is the auto inspection.
Waiting at the station for my rejection.
It's safety I know, but I have an objection.
Couldn't manufacturers try for more perfection.

Cars
I know some folks really love their cars.
Personally, they have left me with scars.
They're a pain to buy, whether used or new.
For registering them, waiting in line makes me stew.
Insurance, especially if you're a young male,
Will cost enough to make you pale.
My personal pain is the annual inspection.
I live in fear of that damned rejection.
Fixing is a frustration that does not stop,
Whether you fix it yourself or go to the shop.
Ending your relationship, cars are hard to sell.
You'd like them to go to the junkyard in hell.
To me they're mechanical jackasses for sure.
All the gadgets included have no allure.
My goal is travel. That's simple and pure.

The Mechanical jackass
Cars are mechanical jackasses I know.
They're nothing more, though they'll knock you low.

Why spend a lot for all the extra stuff?

It will cause you anguish and make life rough.

In time everything breaks, so why ask for trouble.

The probability of needing service will more than double.

So my advice to car owners is this,

Keep cars simple and some trouble you'll miss.

KISS

Keep it simple stupid, or KISS

Applies to all devices. You must know this.

Less complexity means less to break.

So keep it simple for your sanity's sake.

Simplicity

A simple low cost car is what we need.

Will people buy it? No, not the modern breed.

They'd rather impress others. That's their creed.

Nasty Drivers

Some things I've noticed over many a year.

The fact that some drivers are getting more nasty is clear.

I would like it if they showed some concern,

And maybe give other drivers a turn.

It's okay to pause. It won't ruin your day,

By helping someone else get on their way.

Also, blocking intersections results in a big jam.

A little consideration is like breaking a dam.

Make a jam by blocking the other guy.

You've caught yourself. You're not too sly.

12. Maxims (Untitled)

All the maxims should suffice,
They come by the flock.
Some are good advice,
While some are a crock.
Some help us to be nice,
The rest we can mock.

Fortunately, the goal of perfection wasn't always our aim
Since there would be no progress. All would stay the same.
The proposition, "The best that anyone can ever do,
Is determined by the available money and time." Is true.

Don't put off 'til tomorrow what you can do today.
That's 'cause when the sun shines, it's time to make hay.
However, haste makes waste, so not too fast.
We all know we have to make the morning last.

If you don't venture, you don't gain.
A lot of gamblers follow this refrain.
It's easy come, easy go, when they lose.
They don't cry over spilt milk nor sing the blues.

Miss by an inch, miss by a mile,
Is a maxim that makes me smile.
The more likely result, and please don't smirk,
It's close enough for government work.

Early to bed and early to rise
Makes a man healthy, wealthy and wise.
Ben said this and that's no surprise.
Health I'll accept. The rest we revise.
Often the hoi polloi are the early to rise.

The road to hell is paved with good intentions.
This is a maxim that most everyone mentions.
If good intentions have the result that dire,
Where can bad intentions lead worse than brimstone and
fire?

If you spare the rod,
You spoil the child.
He just needs a prod.
You can be more mild.

Absence makes the heart grow fonder.
About this we all may ponder.
Maybe it's out of sight, out of mind,
Perhaps this happens because love is blind.

A moving stone gathers no moss.
Interpreting this saying makes me cross.
Is gathering moss a good thing to do?
If so, playing it safe means sticking like glue.
Or is moss something stagnant and bad,
And you should get moving fast, I might add.
Maybe I'll ignore it and be just as glad.

I've heard that, "Time wounds all heels."
The heel not suffering is the more likely, I feel.
Chances are the cad will get away free.
It's more likely that, and you'll have to agree,
"No good turn goes unpunished," has higher probability.

My friend Izzy, when victimized by a scam,
Replied to me, "Well, that's water under the dam."
"That's water over the bridge, " he also said.
It's mixing his sayings that I most dread.

"People who live in glass houses shouldn't throw stones."
"People who live in grass houses shouldn't stow thrones."
In neither case could they take mortgage loans.
When people read this, I can hear the groans.

A stitch in time, needs a better rhyme.
Like a stitch of mine, would certainly save nine.
One stitch in time, is a science fiction crime.

One component of wisdom, and this can be pretty rough,
Is knowing when to stop and say that's good enough.

If you want perfection, then finish you never will,
No matter your smarts nor your level of skill.

God helps those who help themselves,
But don't take too much and empty the shelves.

Familiarity breeds contempt, is a saying that we should scrap.
It doesn't fit any people I know. Thus, it's full of crap.

"Leave no stone unturned," means be as thorough as you can.
"Leave no tern unstoned," is a practice they should ban.

They say a fool and his money will soon part.
How did he get that money if not too smart?

13. Humor and Backward Bob

It Is I

Knock, knock, "Who's there?" "It's me."

This is wrong as you can see.

"It is I," is correct. Wait a sec or three.

I'm certainly not an it, so, "I am he."

Oh, they all sound strange. Just say, "Lee."

However,

For the plural case, say," They are we," or, "We are they."

To hell with it. Say, "Lee and Ray."

To avoid confusion, say, "Identify yourself please,"

Then there's no worry about I, me, or we's.

Extreme Alliteration

Supposedly silent Simple Simon started saying,

"Someone should stop Sweet Sara's swaying."

Simon saw sick Sara's sudden spews.

Swiftly shifting, Simon saved spattered shoes.

Backward Bob

Backward Bob was always confused by his name.

When spelled backward or forward, it was the same.

He decided backward was better and accepts any blame.

When you hear him, you'll know it's no game.

Untitled Poems

Backward Bob ran fro and to.
He was in a tizzy about what to do.
To help him out, they gave him a smack.
Now he's charging forth and back.

The poor guy suffered from the attack.
Both of his eyes were blue and black.

The weather man had to adjust his stats
When he found it was raining dogs and cats.

I tell you sir, this is a shock.
What you tell me is a crock.
I've never heard such bull and cock.

Backward Bob ran back to front.
He worked so hard he had to grunt.
Then a sailor appeared at the door.
So Bob began running aft and for.

Poor Backward Bob, he is so thin,
He's nothing at all but bones and skin.

We have the cons and pros. What's more,
We need to know those against and for.

Where's Bob? He's about and out.
If you see him, pleases give a shout.

Do you think Bob is at your call and beck?
Don't disturb him. He's relaxing on the deck.

Bob was at a loss for words,
When telling his son about the bees and birds.

Backward Bob has a lunch time wish.
He'd like his favorite, chips and fish.
For dinner he wants some beans and franks,
With butter and bread, he'll give his thanks.

For Bob, an awful lot of time it took,
Since he had check each cranny and nook.
He searched far and near, over dale and hill.
If we hadn't stopped him, he'd be there still.

Don't give me that dance and song.
You think you're right. I think you're wrong.
We were looking for a poor young waif.
After hours, we found him sound and safe.

The traffic was so thick, it was go and stop.
Where are they when you really need a cop?

When we searched, we found neither hair nor hide.
Shall we look down or up? We must decide.

Bob searched everywhere, wide and far.
He was hungry and needed that grill and bar.

They said they could fix Bob's truck or car
After his experience they need feathers and tar.

An American institution that's blue, white, and red,
Is the ubiquitous small inn, the breakfast and bed.

All those dealers of used and new cars
Shouldn't advertize with stripes and stars.

The neighborhood kids all skinny or fat
Played baseball just needing a ball and bat.

Bob just can't begin. He's all starts and fits.
His technique it seems is misses and hits.
The result of course is pieces and bits.

At school, Bob went out for field and track.
After practice he was reduced to ruin and rack.

The life of a carpenter has some glamour.
There's more to it than nail and hammer.

To the stadium all the fans went and came.
They wanted to see the annual Navy-Army game.

The young lovers ran over dale and hill.
They had a special place to coo and bill.

After working hard with shovel and pick,
Bob built a fireplace of mortar and brick.
By the time he finished he was tired and sick.

Bob was found to be true and tried,
So he and his love became groom and bride.

After losing his money on each bond and stock,
Bob was between a hard place and a rock.

The best way to dance to roll and rock,
Is to get on the floor without shoe and sock.

They found the whole band of bugle and drum
Had consumed a great quantity of coke and rum.

Bob became a machinist, the type, die and tool.
When working he is collected, calm, and cool.

Bob's mom kept working through thin and thick.
She'd never rest 'til all was span and spick.

The courts deal with punishment and crime.
Some of their rulings have no reason or rhyme.

"You rotten crook, choose either tail or head.
When I bring you in, you're alive or dead."

Worthwhile play includes games and fun.
Be active and always jump and run.

Exorbitant taxes will do little harm.
All they demand is a leg and an arm.

Backward Bob is about and around.
Wherever we look, he can't be found.

There's mental, emotional, and physical smarts.
A modicum of each, great at crafts and arts.

The famous general even struts in mud.
He often is called old guts and blood.

The amount of work Bob does will astound.
To be successful he is determined and bound.

When Bob works around his place,
His favorite drill is his bit and brace.

Once Bob ate too much. He was a glutton.
He grew so he burst every bow and button.

Bob graduated since he was no sap.
He was all dressed up in his gown and cap.

About cleanliness don't be a dope.
Wash your hands with water and soap.

I don't want to make a liar of you.
So answer the question, false or true.

Bob was asked if he ever ate too much chow.
He answered, "Not often but maybe then and now."

Our government is based on the balance and check.
We should be careful that this we don't wreck.

His sister is like Bob. When she went to the prom,
She danced with all, including Harry, Dick, and Tom.

Bob exercises enough so he stays really trim.
He can start every task with vigor and vim.
When he eats too little, he's as thin as a rail.
So then we see he's not hearty and hail.

When in the military, Bob had to be fit.
His uniform was perfect, all polish and spit.

When I watch Bob, I have to smile.
If he's not sure, it's all error and trial.

She tends to lie, Bob's good friend Ruth.
She doesn't seem to know, it's consequences or truth.

Businessman Bob goes to all sorts of lengths
To find his competitors weaknesses and strengths.

When Bob's friend Tolstoy wished to write some more,
He started a new novel, Peace and War.

Listening to Bob's lawyer, I yawn and sigh.
He tells me everything, every wherefore and why.

Bob is a quiet man, and he has his skill.
He personifies the saying, "Deep waters run still."

The taxpayers are upset by the money they're bleeding.
The schools all complain about what they're all needing.
Both have to push arithmetic, writing, and reading.

Take it easy, poor Bob's had enough.
In fact we're all tired from this tumble and rough.

Poor Bob tripped and landed on his tush.
This is what happens when shove comes to push.

Bob got everyone together to thank.
These were the workers, the file and rank.

Bob will say this to his very last breath.
Nothing is certain in life except taxes and death.

To Bob, what they have in common, is not clear.
These are doctors of throat, nose, eye, and ear.

Why did two showoff males who strip,
Pick innocent names like Dale and Chip?

They seem ignorant, so what's wrong with them?
Why not admit it and not haw and hem?

Don't mess with the devil and raise his ire,
Else you'll spend eternity in brimstone and fire.

In this nursery rhyme, Bob changes the words,
So little Miss Muffet eats her whey and curds.

Bob's a good guy though sometimes he's fresh.
This shows he's a real human of blood and flesh.

The line between them is not so exact.
I'm talking about the difference between fiction and fact.

The ancient Greeks often fought in the buff.
Their enemies knew they were ready and rough.

Sometimes I think Bob has no brain.
He'll try almost anything shine or rain.

There is one drink that's hard to botch.
Bob's special favorite, the soda and scotch.

When you fall into the drink,
You have a choice, swim or sink.

Although Bob was sometimes a souse,
They made him head of grounds and house.

A mode of transportation Bob likes to endorse,
Is the old time favorite, the wagon and horse.

Bob just got his lawyer's exorbitant bill.
He had written Bob's last testament and will.

Bob went to the hospital to visit his wife
Her condition was described as death or life.

After reading the arguments, Bob found the flaw.
It was all a matter of order and law.

When making a serious social gaff,
Bob didn't know whether to cry or laugh.

To this, Bob thinks you should agree.
The philosophy is right, die or live free.

"How much did you win? Was it a big score?"
"Oh around twenty one grand, less or more."

Whether the distance is far or near,
Certainly it's neither, there nor here.

When all is done and said,
I think I'd rather be in bed.

They determine how much tax each pays,
Those committee guys of the means and ways.

A sales technique Bob will always hate,
Is used by some salesman, the old switch and bait.

It's strange how many a famous celeb
Has notoriety that will flow and ebb.

The poor gambler prays to his gods.
His whole life reduces to evens and odds.

A brief lunch meal is salad and soup.
The salad comes first, so it doesn't droop.

Bob's so busy he'll go and come.
We're not sure if it's to or from.

"Do you have this gizmo?" Bob nods.
"It's in my collection of ends and odds."

Bob's friend was charged with battery and assault.
He kept claiming it was not his fault.

The tenant did everything to break the lease.
The judge told him to desist and cease.

I've never heard such cock and bull.
Me thinks of the blarney you are full.
It seems you want my leg to pull.

Bob's in a hurry, so he can't dither.
He has to look all over yon and hither

We all hope for an economic boom.
What we hear is the same old doom and gloom.

What an insensitive thing, your wife to call.
Referring to her as the old chain and ball.

The salad dressing you will spoil,
If you try to mix your vinegar and oil.

In the lifetime game between dolls and guys,
He who cares the most, gets the prize.

In our unit we had a pretty nice sarge.
He didn't care if we were small or large.

During the Spring, there was a foul weather spell.
We found a new comparison: high water or hell.

To Bob and his wife, nothing has more wonder
Than to witness a storm with lightening and thunder.

Bob counts on his toes and fingers.
When he gets up to twenty, he lingers.
He decides to use each foot and hand.
His new system seems pretty grand.

Our Molly is such an active pup,
She spends her time jumping down and up.
If she gets away, she's quite a rover,
Any obstacle, she squirms under or over.

Our great country, wrong or right.
Sometimes we just have to fight.

They made the trek, did Lewis and Clark.
In American history, they sure made their mark.
Why not Clark and Lewis to share the fame?
Must we keep the usual order of names?

In the old days a popular show was Andy and Amos.
We listened regularly, and who could blame us.

There were two siblings Abel and Cain.
Poor Abel by his brother was slain.

If I could have the perfect with,
It would be for health of kin and kith.

"I'm going out." "It's raining out there.
Get an umbrella or something to wear."
"The wind may blow. The rain may pelt.
I will not rust, nor will I melt."

You have ants in your bonnet
Or bees in your pants.
I could write a sonnet
When I see you dance.

People named orange and lemon, I've known more than one.
But of grapefruit, tangerine, and lime, there are none.

Some is written by the poet.
It's said, some will throw it.
It's used widely to grow it.
It's bull, and we all should know it.

If in doubt,
Holler and shout.
If you want your way,
Bellow and bray.
If you know you can't,
Then rave and rant.
If you don't behave,
I'll rant and rave.
When you're all alone,
Groan and moan.